To Doris

May you enjoy

Esther

Moments Between

by
Esther C. Asmus

illustrated by
Nancy L. Siniff

published by
Country Messenger Press

Moments Between

Edited by Sol Squire

Printed in the United States of America

Published by
The Country Messenger Press
16022 Oakhill Road North
Marine on St. Croix, MN   55047

ISBN 0-9619407-2-7

In dedication to my husband,

Harold William Asmus

May 1, 1920 - November 28, 1987,

who added dearly and richly to my life

who taught me to need what is worthwhile
                    to live in warmth, kindness and comfort
                    to learn with courage, humility and confidence
                    to trust in integrity, strength and loyalty

who taught me that meaning in life
                    can be cherished like a fine wine
                    and will save our dreams

for the years of our marriage
November 27th, 1941 - November 28th, 1987

Forward

There are universal concerns. Even though all of us are different in very fundamental ways, there are still common needs and hopes we all share. This is a book of uncomplicated poetry written in plain english which hopes to touch those common elements in all of us.

The world, our world, seems to change hourly. The experiences of one generation cannot be expected to be valid for the next. Yet always there will be the joys of Nature, the need to deal with both the very good and very unfortunate circumstances of our lives in a graceful manner.

A very real part of our modern lives is alienation. We, more than any other people before us, live in little boxes. Our families tend to fracture at the first chance offered: parents living alone and children hundreds of miles away. We have to adjust. This is a book of adjustment and the appreciation of adjustment.

This is an American book, written in the Upper-Midwest. The values and concerns harbored here are those of the Heartland. So much of what we do and don't do is based more on attitude than any other factor. It is our state of mind that separates being alone from loneliness or defines the moment when crisis end and recovery begins. The patterns of attitude which reflect our individual values take time for others to recognize, unless you write a book.

Here is the pattern of one life which, like any natural thing, has been colored and shaped by a thousand influences. The expression of this pattern is a mosaic in which all of us should find a few familiar hues.

Sol Squire

Table of Contents

Table of Contents

Moments Between

Our new abode
　　shall harbor no death
Eternal love darkness
　　cannot abide
Earthly passings are only
　　the moments between
Steps on a journey
　　to with Him reside

When you open the door
What do you expect to find?
Surely something magic
Hid suspensefully behind

If the door were ajar
And you could peek around
In a sliver of light
What might be found?

Often welcome beckons
And most excitedly we are
To follow the enticement
Either near or very far

Nothing there but darkness
Mystery! We delay!
Need we really enter?
Perhaps tomorrow — not today

I go to my church
    my God is there
    He is the Host
        of the House of God
    He is there

I wake at the break of day
    my God is there
    so full of certainties
        so mystical and calm
    He is there

I trod down my twisting path
    my God is there
    giving me courage at each step
        giving me strength and fortitude
    He is there

I ask for forgiveness and for peace
    my God is there
    He gives me release from blanketing grief
        The sadness dries to joy
    He is there

I close my eyes in prayer at night
    my God is there
    I thank Him for the radiance of this day
        I ask for comfort through the night
    He is there

I know I cannot be alone
    my God is there
    my soul is guarded with His eternal care
        and there is no wealth outside of Him
    He is there

I looked into a muddied pool
     and saw a field of cloudless blue sky

I found a chunk of dry crusty bread
     and enjoyed a gourmet's banquet

I walked down a corridor so very dark
     and was guided by the illumination of truth

I took in a bird with a broken wing
     and it flew with the wind to the Port of Heaven

I heard the sobs of a broken heart
     and mended it with bandages of compassion

I saw the struggle of the scrawny shrub
     and sent its roots into veins of rich soil

I shared the ebony visions a blind man holds
     and found a courageous art without frame

I walked in the desert hot and parched
     and saw it bloom in flowers of hope

I encountered the heartache of a soul confused
     and found an island of faith for a purpose sublime

I was the door, the armory, the anchor
     to serve with an intention pure
     to inspire with a spiritual weapon
     to steady the helm in a storm of temptation

May I then, God, be the canvas
     over which Your colors flow
     reflecting Your brush's vigor
     and inspiring all who choose to see Your art

What did I do today?
I walked and spoke with Him

The morning's newness brought
          birth to thoughts and hopes
While waking under an infinite
          tender sky
With a morning haze on the horizon
          I yearned for the sun's light
Relishing the wondrous bud
          of this day's birth
I prayed that the wings of love
          would kiss the snow
                    on wrinkled brows and
          hope would gleam
                    in the youthful hearts
I asked with eagerness
          that we might all be
                    friends bonded in trust
          that the bowls of the hungry
                    would fill to the brim
          the journey would cease
                    for those searching for a home
          that the earth would find balance in
                    justice, mercy and humility
          and that forever lost would be the fears
                    and sorrows in the heart of a child

I prayed that world's hopes would
          reflect faith into corridors dim
That the world set aside the
          half-truths, ignorance and morbid doubts
That good hearts, truth, faith and ready hands
          would weave a pattern of harmony
                    into the fabric of time

I prayed that laughter will
　　　in every brook flow
That all smiles linger
　　　just a bit longer
That the music of the soul
　　　would find greater harmonies
That it be revealed for all to see
　　　there is no death;
　　　　　just immortality

And so the time passed for us as
I walked and spoke with Him

WEALTH

Wealth is not
    an accounting of money
    acres of real estate
    name on the social registry
    or travels to relate

Wealth is the
    care from a loving family
    trust of a child in need
    the concern of a good neighbor
    memories of a kind deed

Wealth is knowing
    our friends are ours to keep
    tomorrow the sun will color the dawn
    that a day of toil will end
    we've made the world better before we're gone

LANDS AFAR

Travel has been a part of my life
It's brought much value and gain
Like stories from a living book
Memories forever for me to retain

Travel gives one an understanding
There is a corner other than one's own
Culture and beauty are seen in a different light
From canyon bottom to mountain throne

Travel displays God's given beauty
The human drama — other nation's ways
All these lands bound somehow together
All looking for peace, a peace that stays

Words
Are the part of life
With which one can express
Ones needs, ones feelings
All rights to happiness

Words
Are the part of us
Our friends learn to know
Our living in actions
May other things show

Words
Are the parent's wish
A newborn's given right
From weak cries of need
To words of truth's might

Words
Stand as our humanity
The link to one's mind
We are given option
To offend or be kind

Words
Have won kingdoms
For the skillful users do know
That well chosen words
Can hide as well as show

Words
Capture a language
And are simple to trade
From culture to culture
As differences fade

NEWNESS OF TOMORROW

Where there is faith
life cannot fail
Where there is love
happiness shall prevail

In lightness of heart
sadness will depart
With joy victorious
life has a new start

As time eases pain
relief replaces sorrow
Faith, hope and love
begin anew tomorrow

SKY'S WONDROUS MAGNITUDE

God opened the skies
Just for me
And spread the clouds
So I could see

Into the endlessness
Of the pastel blue shell
The perfect smooth curve under which
All life must dwell

With my breath held for seconds
My heart filled by the blue so spare
Even in the empty above me, I knew
Where there's nothing, He's there

Walking down a country road
In the morning at ten below
The awesome beauty of frost overtook me
And I had to stop for a minute or so

Unblemished was the tranquil softness
Encasing the forested north
The white perfection of fleeting caprice
Etched a picture of immeasurable worth

Above was an infinity of shallowest blue
Here on earth the white of snow and stony grey lake
The shadowy outline of black 'neath the boughs
Was a framework of calm other seasons forsake

The changes of contour and rounding of edge
Ended the twistings of twig and barbed wire
All was clad in a fur of pure ice
Sculpted without hands and forged without fire

No living thing moved
Or touched the frost which had grown
Who'd disturb this perfection
Where God's breath had blown?

The snows had ceased
The winds had stilled
The sun in glory reigned

In the still of winter-land
I trod
I listened
          noises were almost muffled
          a Pileated hammered for sustenance
          a chain's buzz in the distance
                    perhaps gnawing for warmth

No other, only
          my footsteps
          with depth all their own

But in numbers
          laced in millions
                    diamonds glisten
                    diamonds sparkle
                              as cut glass sprinkled on cotton
                              such brilliance blinding
Had I found another reality?

To console my eyes
I rested
          in the printed shadow of
          a branching image

Then they bolted
          before me
          across my path
                    a rabbit deftly leapt
                    a deer arced forward

And with my human feet
     did I invade
     I felt I was the intruder
        stepping most timidly
        that I might not disjoin

What had fallen before me
What had charmed the land
As the stars in the heaven
     caught in the light of their sparkle-dance
       Diamonds in the snow

WINTER'S WALK

'Tis a wintery afternoon
But like a breath of finest springtide air
Weighing each dewy fragment carefully
And in January, most very rare

The fallen snow has firmed to steel
Glistening like tinsel on a bough
Daringly I move in measured step
Wishful not to stumble or lose my balance somehow

And just as footprints made anew
Puddles pout in watery dismay
Could I have been a month in sleep
And awoke to find a world in spring grey?

But does it really matter
This change in winter's mystery
A warmer tomorrow will come soon enough
I return to winter's reality

NEW MORN

With dawn the morning,
Day is born anew
A quiet common miracle
Allowing thoughts to renew

Our hopes rush to consciousness
As the unseen dews of dawn first shine
Off leaves and water-rounded stones
The leap of sun above the horizon's line

At last we celebrate the rebirth
Winter's end felt within
Breathtaking April awaits in the wings
    slowly in a ritual step
        makes her entrance

April whose young fragrance
    lingers between the raindrops
    and loosens the green and gold belt
    of her daffodil robe

April touches the earth from beneath
    pushing to life inquiring shoots
    her velvet green gloves leaving fingerprints
    which mark the evidence of Spring

Spring is reborn
    in a veil of pale green
    the first birth of the year
    baptized in dew

SHARED COLORS

That tiny garden of the spectrum
    the roses
    the gladiolus
        the same light reflect
And in all their various forms
    rework the shared colors

In orchards and vineyards
    blossoms waft tender petals
    daisies beg at tree's feet
        in a language unspoken
The vibrant reef of a billion hues
        each perfect for a time

TODAY

Waste not today
Hardly a moment to spare
Take the time to look around
And see that God is everywhere

Beauty is budding
You can pick a bouquet
Take in the scent of Heaven
And in your memory let it stay

Today is the treasure
Polish the hours bright
Let the sparkle of your living
Bring to all eyes a delight

And refrain from all worry
At the close of a day
The darkness which follows
Must to dawn give way

Miss Reba Rabbit went to shop
And to a friend Miss Reba said,
"What I want and really need
Is a Spring bonnet for my head"

But, oh, so many on the shelf
Pink, lavender and blue trimmed lace
Soon Reba became all adither
As hat by hat went above her face.

But what would Peter Rabbit like
It is him, her love, she wanted to please
On Fifth Avenue they would stroll
And she wanted to be the only one he sees

Peter's favorite color all these years
Had consistently been sky blue
So that choice she wisely made
Squinching her nose, as rabbits do

Now you can see the two of them
Paw in paw strolling Easter Day
He's telling her how fine she looks
The very words she wants him to say

In the morning
There is haste
Those hours few of early day
Not a time to waste

We have this affair
This orb and I
Who is known to most
The Old Man in the Sky

With red fingers he beckons
He directs me to the East
We turn in full welcome
Every man, bird and beast

And then the bell tolls
Children called to a school day
He's high above the horizon
A signal — no delay!

Yes, we have a love affair
This Old Man and I
And we'll meet again tomorrow
It's a love that'll never die

Outside my bedroom window
On a dewy summer morn
They beckon me to
Come to the glass
And open it

Fervent warbling throats
They sing to one another
Announcing the birth of a summer day
The first of only too few

My curtains part
My eyes feast
All about is a wooded green
The tree tops wave
The low plants stretch
A carpet of emerald flows

On their branches the callers sit
The white birch most elegant
A dipping flitter of a solo flyer
The old oak so very gnarled
The world outside is awakening
And I can feel the breath of Life

CHALLENGE OF A TREE

There's a contest in the forest
Like humanity is in form
Each tree has its calling
To shelter and to warm

The forest like a city
Grows clusters, short of space
Each tree to outclimb the other
They must endure this global race

Some grow stately to command
Others slightly bend to heed
Some easily give up the struggle
Some survive but always need

PRAYING

Praying is a part of us
It is done in various ways
Some feel the need of bended knee
While others sing words of praise

Some feel the need of a temple
Or a church's walls of strength
Some feel only in private
Can one make confessions at length

There are the ones who walk in the wood
Letting only the tree tops hear
The prayer of honest thankfulness
Private time to let go a tear

Others pray throughout the day
In all matters they hold dear
Feeling the presence of the Lord
In their lives He's always near

Each dawn is an eruption of
Expectations. Hopes and dreams unwind;
The flowering of achievement new
Can further stretch the mind

Each morning is a dedication
The curtain rising on Life's stage
Red with sharpest anticipation
The dawn turns night's inked page

Each morning is the dawn of another birthday
With a gift of future hours
A painted sky of shifting hues
Cries out the majesty of God's powers

A CHILD'S MORNING PRAYER

Dear God, it's me, the tiny one
I love You very much
I love my family, father, mother
But I love You more than any other

Dear God, would you ask Your Son
To watch over me through the day
Let me play in Your sunshine
And teach me to be a child of Thine

Dear God, I'm sure You've noticed
I'm growing and getting wiser
And as I grow the more I know
That endless is the love You show
                    Thank you, Lord

I love You

When God stopped by this morning
He walked throughout my garden
And turned the darkness with a crimson sun
Hung the white lacy clouds in place one by one
Then dried the dewdrops on the petal's pearled edge
And authored the song in a robin's breast
A great melody rushed up the valley walls
Carried by gentle breezes sporting over the slopes
Calling out that another day of destiny is born

The harborer of all grace and beauty
He strolled among the green furrows
As He brushed His robe on the budding stems
There appeared a tapestry of petals
And all the tiny ones who live in dark places
Came forth, each a beauty of creation
And shared the fragrances of an earthly dawn
As He and I reached the garden's edge

Are you as grateful as I
This day did not pass you by?

Each blossom shares the same destiny as a star

Each flower's colors as fresh as new oils on canvas

Each cluster perfumed with the intangible

Each petal reveals the divine hand

My garden grows in the earth of splendor

VACATION

Today I'll pack my bag
And leave this place, my home
I'll make my way to places unknown
Over mountain peaks and ocean foam

Those who stay will say I left
For a much deserved vacation
I never need much reason
For a trip to another nation

Though the trail be short or very long
Some adventure I'm sure to find
Let me walk the rolling sphere
Satisfy my inquiring mind

There's knowledge out there for me to reap
Which books have missed in harvests past
I'll go and go 'til the horizon ends
And then turn for home, my home, at last

Sand. Wave worn, tossed but unhurt
Soft drifted mounds; the hem on land's skirt

Oh, sugary bits of mindless rocks
A seat for contemplation, a road for long walks

It has given the young a wealth of joy
The children scoop with shovel and toy

Young and old have built castles of sand
Hours in construction, for minutes they stand

The beaches, elegant and very proud
Defy the wave and stormy dark cloud

The sandy foundations of lovers' dreams
Made possible when lit by moonbeams

Swimmers know the firm feeling of sand
Where the beach lies and safety's at hand

The shifting sand beckons those who need rest
Watch the setting sun and gulls without nest

Sand. Wave worn, tossed but unhurt
Soft drifted mounds; the hem on land's skirt

Sand. Wave worn, tossed but unhurt
Soft drifted mounds; the hem on land's skirt

My summer porch
        a delightful sanctuary
                washed with bright
                early rays of sun
                        where moonlight
                        haunted between screened walls
                                and starshine tumbled
                                like a spray of precious jewels

        enjoying in the
                season of Spring
                        my lilac trees
                        aged and tall
                                my hands touch not
                                their bloom at all
                                        they call the bees
                                        with perfume sent
                                                before their blossoms
                                                relent to summer's rains

No secrets are hid
        among the
                shadowed tree boughs
                        framed spaces recall what was
                                of midnight bonfires
                                fishing boats
                                sails full
                                storms upon the
                                        wavy surface

        it is all revealed to me
                through checkered screens
                        polka-dots of dust
                        coagulated in the tiny crossed wires
                                the dust of candle soot
                                the dust kicked up by summer rains

The white wicker
    of olden years
        offers me comfort
            how sad it is
            to know they cannot pass
            these moments on in their creakings
                nor will their loosened strands
                twist to write this
                story for those who come later

What stories they might tell
    of the words exchanged
        of the scandalous
        of the good of heart
        of the wicked and the gallant
            the flirtatious glances
            the passions revealed
            dancing and dueling
                now all silent, now all grey

All that would be
    a true history
        of lives with their
        twists and turns
            history not in books
            but of a truer vintage
            mellowed as memories for years
                recalled as the "olden times"

Oh, cobweb in the window
    greeting the morning sun
Oh, cobweb in the window
    the morning works' begun
Oh, cobweb in the window
    like lace, you have been spun
Oh, cobweb in the window
    greeting the morning sun

Oh, cobweb in the window
    where were you yesterday
Oh, cobweb in the window
    you must not plan to stay
Oh, cobweb in the window
    where did your builder stray?
Oh, cobweb in the window
    where were you yesterday?

Oh, cobweb in the window
    I cannot care for thee
Oh, cobweb in the window
    I plan to set you free
Oh, cobweb in the window
    Others won't your beauty see
Oh, cobweb in the window
    I cannot care for thee

With agile necks
      and worldly trust
They tip their heads
      and lightly dream
Between pointed ears
      It's nappin' time

Paws overlapping or
      tucked beneath
Furred soft bodies
      dream silently
          peacefully
      It's nappin' time

I shall not wake
      nor rudely interrupt
My Gent
My Lady
      in their repose
      It's nappin' time

Though of feline breed
      they, such as we
Truly need
      the gentle pause
          quiet, serenity
      It's nappin' time

Fog
  is that
  parenthesis
    between
    the sun
    the light
    the dry
    the wet

It bleeds into resistant spaces

And obscures the trail
  of a billion stars

It devours the fields
Grays the slow breeze
Smells of things earthy and unseen

As the clearer world
  is wrapped in this errant cloud
All is washed away
  like colored chalk from a sidewalk

Unlike ice
  it does not reflect the sun
Unlike the sea
  it does not thunder in waves

It stretches gnawing
  feelings
My inner fears nudge me
  Let it stay out there

Alluring and alone

the poppy stands

on wiry stem

hairy leafed

flamboyant in orange red

a spectacular showing

an etude of elegance

dormant lie

comrades

deep under cover

darkness persists

how long will

the poppy last

before

nature's calling

to end

the withering

      alone. . . . . .

What is a farmer?
    A man in a coat of tan
        in the Summertime
    A man with a wind blown face
        in the Wintertime
    A man most anxious
        in the Spring of the year
    But Fall is the season
        to bring joy or a tear

A farmer
    is a man known by various names
        the dumb farmer
        the gentleman farmer
        the cattle farmer
        the wealthy farmer
        the owner of the land

Whatever his name
    whatever his station
        because of his toil
            we have our ration

May it be milk from the cow
    or the fruit from the hen
        without the Farmer
            our table would be
                quite barren

When we, the city folk,
    are comfy and clean
There are times the farmer
    has not our esteem
He is the man
    whose work never ends
He is the laborer
    on which all depends

A cornstalk leans in the harvest moon
A pumpkin ripe on a serpentine vine
The mice of field gnaw on anxious thoughts
A clear night of owlish light

The moon casting a stony tone
As crisp as a new fallen leaf
So still, so calm, so quiet and waiting
Rest all living things under the harvest moon

Brooks and streams run like excited mercury
The woods are alive with anonymous sound
All eyes are wide open and ears straining hard
Waiting for this witchcraft to end with the dawn

The boiling of a storm of reds
Each leaf as rich as a glass of wine
The burning blush of the maple
Embarassed to say good bye

Branches afire with fingers of ruby
Hiss at the wind with burning anger
One by one they turn and depart
And face to the ground they await the snow

At the height of their beauty their time has come
The calendar sees no justice for them
A tiny few are pressed between yellowing pages
As an echo of the moment they fell

They now blanket the earth at their mother's feet
A thin protection from the mindless snow
As autumn fades their embarassment lessens
And hidden from view they silently yield

A good summer
having come to an end

likens to the
loss of a special friend

From tiny country cabins
From homes on valley slopes
To city grey stone mansions
To wherever dwell human hopes
Is where Santa heads, his great bag full
In a polished sled which reindeer pull
Knowing
Goodness Has Never Been Better

Homes all tidy with scents of spice
Polished glass reflects the glow
Of log fires set in an ancient hearth
And the Star above from long ago
And made with every hope to please
Are feasts from old family recipes
Knowing
Goodness Has Never Been Better

An air of electric excitement
Keeps children awake in their beds
A few lay with eyes closed pretending
Letting hopes run wild in their heads
And above, far above in clear winter skies
Speeds the jolly man with twinkling eyes
Knowing
Goodness Has Never Been Better

Toys stuffed and trains electric
Mark the festive season
The reds and greens of adorned trees
The choir's Kyrie Eleison
Gratefulness is magicly wrought
The toil of the year almost forgot
Knowing
Goodness Has Never Been Better

In a thousand traditions
In lands so far away
People join with their loved ones
The older plan, the children play
Christmas joys have kept still for a year
The time is at hand, happily we're
Knowing
Goodness Has Never Been Better

We'll remember with kindness the
kindred spirits of joy
the honest desire for peace
and know wealth gained from
joyful yuletide hearts

May we hold some of the love given
to us this Christmas season
passing the rest on to another
and another and another

May the elder tell of
and the child anticipate
a life so beautiful
that dreams become
more than thoughts
realized

May you and I trust in
the lasting beauty, joy
and friendship

Which we so treasure in
this gracious Season
passing into a New Year

Proclaim Peace to All
Good Will to Men

I watch the Christmas tree depart

All that preciousness collected
   adornments, salutations, Santas
   stored away for another year

My heart breaks a little

My heart's tears flow

If only the Season's Spirit knew
   how much it was loved
   what joy it brought
   what memories will be recounted
   how in our hearts it will live on

The rooms seem vacant
   no more sparkling chatter
   no more bright packages of mystery
   no more Christmas melodies

Our home seems suddenly empty
   clean and uncluttered
   emptied of shared feelings

All is packed away
   and we resume life
   with a lingering Christmas Spirit
   mindful of The Promise
   hoping for realized dreams

Now we can fold up this Christmas;
   an old, scented letter we can
   tuck in the envelope of our hearts

It's a sullen day
    one so dispirited
        so cold
        grayed steel
        winded in sharp icicles
Firmly corseted in leadened dimness

Grateful are we
    for the bundled layers
        of garments
        to wrap and re-wrap
        rescue our bodies
        from the bluing bruising
Awarded by the bitterness of the winter cold

The clouds in control
    have suppressed the sun
        now that day's nearing end
        there's a bit of relenting
        the tireless sun piercing through

Yes, there in the sky
    held by greater, unknown forces
        appears a slice of the sun
        pale in color
        scant in dimension

Like a slice of lemon
    a thin slice of lemon
    palest of lemon

It rests in the lower sky
    as if humbled and about to glide
    over the shadowed edge of evening

The sun has shone
    though feeble
    austere in dignity
    a moment of yellow
        the fulfillment of a daily promise

JUDGE NOT

It is not a profile that describes a man
Or stature short or tall
Rather the character from within the soul
Which to others means most of all

It is not how man may cast his wealth
Or keep it in vaults apart
So long as for what and to whom
It is given, it's given from the heart

Some men prefer a castle
Or other stone domain
And there are those who comfort find
Within a cottage plain

As the wise so long ago said
"Judge not a book by its cover"
It is in knowing one's fellow man's soul
That a hidden treasure we'll discover

SHORT GAL'S LAMENT

Have you seen this year's fashions?
So dull, so big, out of proportion?
They're atrocious, wouldn't you say?
I'd rather they were part of yesterday.

For you, the young, willowy and tall
They are lovely — such style and grace
However, I sing the Short People song
These fashions and I do not get along

Yes, for you gals long and stately
These fashions will be of benefit greatly
We shorties must sigh and hope that some day
The worship of altitude will soon go away

MINDFUL

One needs not lose sight to be blind
Blindness is obstruction of mind
What can be ours if we care to see
The charge isn't much; often it's free

Of the world so real about us
Touching, nudging, so gently and thus
To see and know we need only observe
Follow roads straight and bend as the way curves

Live life boldly and see His intent
Enjoy the fullest what from above has been lent

CITY

I look out a window
At rooftops in Summer swelter
What secrets beneath are held
The dramas they must shelter

Aged buildings large and small
Massive, stately and strong
Keep watch over each other
Deaf to the wind's idle song

Some in wood — some in brick
Some in black — some in white
Structures of harmony
Cold guardians of might

I pass each day with gratitude
     though stumble I may,
     safely I'll move through another day
With God by my side
     my direction takes me where His light goes
     on a path lined with lily and rose
My life is one of gratitude

I live each day in gratitude
     rejoicing in splendor of the earth
     accepting the suffering needed for birth
With God by my side
     dreams awaiting in my soul
     may they walk forth like a new-born foal
My life is one of gratitude

I touch each day in gratitude
     to see the morn and night forget
     and greet the sun without regret
With God by my side
     my life's hopes navigate the sharpest turning
     of the course He sets and sees me learning
My life is one of gratitude

I offer comfort each day in gratitude
     may hearts so weary, lonely and sad
     respond to the lessons that I've had
With God by my side
     may they awake to every tomorrow
     rising triumphant above their sorrow
My life is one of gratitude

Create for me spaces
And a world without walls
Oh, don't bolt door or window
I need the sunset and bird calls

Others are out there
Great numbers have banded
Noah's great ship
Here must have landed

Please, no concrete paths
Or shell-bordered trails
I need the outdoors
Where Nature's love never fails

Everything leafed or legged
Lives a pattern of its own
Together deep in emerald meadows
Or on grey peaks, all alone

Had God not made me human
I with them might have soared
Or galloped or leapt or slithered
But I'm me, thank the Lord

LIFE'S INTEGRITY

Surely no rumor
    did you spread today
God gave you a tongue
    to speak another way

If you repeated hearsay
    were your words really true?
Is it your given right
    to be accuser and judge too?

Give it some thought
    Is your closet truly clean?
So many hide discomforts
    and stoop in shame unseen

With books so full of knowledge
    the world so filled with song
Observe, absorb and listen
    True character is strong

DID I OFFEND

Did I offend in any way?
I didn't hear from you today

Something's happened, you're offended
If unkind, it was not what I intended

Accept my love, as I do you
My heart remains; my feelings true

No doubt, the fault rests with me
I felt too busy to take time to see

The love you offer, it's always there
Close or far, I know you care

Time slips by at so swift a pace
Too long since I have seen your dear face

Did things today not go so well?
Do you hope for a brighter tomorrow?
Will there be suffering you might ease
Or an offer of peace, comfort for sorrow?

Was this day a total waste?
Who controlled the reason?
The choices made, they were your own
Beauty and happiness know no season

Perhaps the chances missed are calling
You to see the need to give
That peace so great within your heart
And a better world to all impart

IF I COULD

If I could this day live over
If I could resay my words
If I could remove my harshness
And replace them with signs of love

If I could relive the moments
If I could recapture yesterday
If I could forget my anger
And replace them with signs of love

If I could remove stains of sadness
If I could scent the odor of gloom
If I could retrace my footsteps
And replace them with signs of love

Then so aware I would be! A day of living
From a heart gracious, in love giving
Of hours enriched with memories filling
The lesson is there, if I am willing

The word Gossip
    should never be heard

It is untruth
    It is not a kind word

Only the unkind
    find the need they repeat

The unthinking words
    that run swift with deceit

What honesty gains
    through words that inspire

Secreted words of attack
    unkindness soon fire

The word Gossip
    should never be heard

It is untruth
    Thus, not a kind word

It is in living that we love
It is in loving that we live

Now that the day's over
What do we have to show?
Was it complete in happiness?
Did we feel our inner-selves grow?

In what manner did we spend it?
Is it one we shall remember?
In what way will life reflect
Those moments rough or tender?

Did we fill someone's need?
Did our hand in help extend?
Did our words and acts of comfort
Pain console and bruises mend?

Are the memories for our album
Ones in later years to come
The kinds of pictures we will treasure
Drawn in beauty — dearly handsome?

May this day have lessened our doubts
And may wisdom grow within our heart
The strength of song — the wealth of hope
Mementos — may they never part

His stay was so brief at
Eleven years of age
And in the story of our lives
He wrote a special page

With candy in hand
This dark-eyed lad
Talked of jaguars and lorries
And the fish he'd had

As young as he was
He had traveled so broad
His father's in the Queen's Navy
The facts kept us awed

He loved his mother so very much
And in their hearts alone
They shared a dream, those two
Of a home they'd call their own

He desired two gifts
For mum and dad at sea
For her there'd be flowers
And for him the finest taffy

We heard of the Big Dipper's thrill
And learned it was a carnival ride
He spoke of engineers and machines
And swelled with British pride

Fish and chips were his favorite
As for any English lad
The taste of cola or skim milk
He thought especially bad

In following his father
He'd taken ship, car and plane
And he thought the tropics his cup of tea
Disliking England's wetness and rain

His memory will be with us
This young adventurer brave
And we can only hope he realizes
The pleasure that he gave

LOVE

Love is masterful
    Love is proud
        Love pervades the universe
Spreading like a cloud

Love can be beautiful
    Love helps us adapt
        Love is a gift
Which is daily unwrapped

MARRIAGE BLESSINGS

With the granting of His blessings
And as He has so willed
The Heavenly union is completed
And a promise is fulfilled

With their families' blessings
In the shelter of parents' pride
Life offers them a future rich
Love's knot forever tied

The blessings of true friends
Beneath the flower, a sturdy stem
Love has a wealth of beauty
The world belongs to them

Our child, our child
Our beautiful child
Your gaze is on us
Only days since you first smiled

We cherish you unendingly
As a gift from above
There's no way to tell you
Of the depth of this love

You will grow so quickly
It seems so unfair
Yet we'll always be happy
He has answered our prayer

The most beautiful picture in all the land
Is the grasp of a child holding the parent's hand

Have you ever traveled
To the place above the cloud
Where the souls with which we're endowed
Are always allowed?

Have you ever traveled
To that wondrously beautiful land
Walking with God on Time's sand
And knowing the warmth of His hand?

Have you ever traveled
By just trusting in a star
To get somewhere so far
That only God knows where you are?

Have you ever traveled
To an island in the sea
Where only happiness can be
To sit beneath His tree?

Yes, we all shall someday travel
Every soul that's ever been
On the wings of angels unseen
To a place that's always green

If I be bared
    from worldly things
I have a memory
    that forever brings
The joy of having
    lived with you and
A love that remained
    forever true

I have watched you
    through another day
Not one moment
    did you stray
From Life's exertions
    and demands
You've been consistent
    through the fall of Time's sands

When another of your days
    is finally done
It gently ends
    you owe no one
An explanation of
    an unkind deed
For only kindness
    did you seed

Lush
      soft as velvet
      burgundy wine of
         the last rose
            lingering
            wants not
               the agony
      of fading forever

Fragrant
      as the finest
      perfume of Paris
         the last rose
            remains
            wants not
               the unknown
      of fading forever

Exquisite
      as lovers' faith
      charming as spring
         the last rose
            defying
            wants not
               the darkness
      of fading forever

Rich
      as rarest gift
      the joy of existence
         the last rose
            rebels
            wants not
               the agony
      of fading forever

We are long remembered
By our word and our deed
Our worth will be known
By values we seed

We each have learned
Through lessons painful and sweet
Life's not meant to be easy
But there's no retreat

God gave us the privilege
To love and to live
God gave us the duty
To earn and to give

Our arms were given
To shelter and extend
To welcome and comfort
The needs of a friend

Our eyes were implanted
All beauty to see
For it's here, all about us
It's endless and free

Our ears are to gather
The sounds of good news
To harken to teachings
And wiser folk's views

Through life we may travel
Our destination far
And in the art of living
May we come to know who we are

It was November of Forty-one
When God, in wisdom, said
"I'll loan to you your husband
On this blessed day you wed

He'll bring to you honor and joy
Which words can't fully express
And gladden all your wedded days
In love, dreams met and happiness"

We lived life for each other
We walked from day to day
In a garden of our love's tending
On a path from which we'd not stray

The years so vibrant did hasten
They numbered but too few
As you, dear, God planned another morn
The Lord made a place for you

That day angels did come for him
No more time could he remain
And so fast he left, the loan now due
We knew someday there'd be this pain

In November of Eighty-seven
Mourning him with my love
Angels came to take him back
To the cloudless home above

I WISH I COULD HAVE GONE WITH HIM

Morning outside
    dreary, cold
    wettish
        we breakfast
        as usual
            oatmeal
            skim milk
            toast

A word or two and we
    relive
        past days
        beautiful days
        friends, families

We plan
    as usual
        our day
            shop
            flowers, a gift
            their new baby
            so much to do

the icicles
    hanging
the morning paper
    waiting
not the day for a drive
    so he walks,
    never to return,
    from his loved home

            his gasp
            the screams
                no one hears
                    the line crackles
                    911 listens

the brave men
the sirens
    the lights
        all mechanical
           chrome and plastic tubes

though hard they try
    he is gone
nothing worked
    death again triumphant

all loved treasures
    earthly
all matters
    relinquished

I know death
    (only a word)
    did not conquer
        God extended His hands

I close my eyes
    the vision is there
    his profile
        unruly lock of hair
        hands clasped behind back

What had he done
    left undone
What shall I do
    we had talked about a plan
Now the loneliness
    the aloneness

I am cold and frozen
I wish I could have gone with him

WHEN GOD COMES TO CALL

Death is only
     the in-between
The shadow of earth
     under Heaven's wall
The threshhold of
     His blessed peace
On the day when
     God comes to call

Beyond Heaven's
     glowing horizon
The bright and welcoming
     waves of light crest
And beckon to us
     to let loads fall
To strain no more
     but take weightless rest

All troubles and
     hurts left behind
Never to enter
     this golden vale
No discord shall ever
     echo here
For the peace of God
     shall never fail

Our new abode
     shall harbor no death
Eternal love darkness
     cannot abide
Earthly passings are only
     the moments between
Steps on a journey
     to with Him reside

Be freed of all toil
     on that parting day
Doubt's rivers shall dry up
     and Fear's mountains shall fall
All the love you have lived in
     will lift you away
On the day when
     God comes to call

They came to weep
They came to love
They gave their strength
    These, our priceless friends
    Thank you, Lord

They came to accept
They came to understand
They gave their concern
    These, our priceless friends
    Thank you, Lord

They came to talk
They came to listen
They gave their comfort
    These, our priceless friends
    Thank you, Lord

Love that is spoken
    is never as intent
As love unspoken
    with deed that is meant

PUBLIC MOMENTS

My steps are untrue
My life passes unmarked
My inside is washed in
        warm salted tears
My once shared dreams
        are now gone, with him

I try not to think
        and then the walls fall
My spirit is black
        with rage
And when my fury
        is spent
I sink into apathy
        from weakness
As my life's blood
        is all squeezed away

Another needed gathering and
        I have little choice
With silent prayer
        upon my lips

In the cold depth
        of chance survival
I try to quell
        my agony gripped heart
As friends extend
        their golden hands
                in a grasp sincere
They say
        "you're taking this
                so very well"

Angry waves
        dig furrows deeper
I need his caress
        my being is wounded

I fight the force of gravity
        and smile
        to hide
        in public moments

I will not say
    "Good-bye" for now

You are not dead
    as you live on
        through your spirit
        in me

I feel your being
    touching me

I hear your voice
    speaking to me

I feel you
    in all the places we rested

I know your
    presence watching me
        as I wander down
        our favorite paths

You are the magnet
    that attracts
        me to Heaven

The light of day brings glistening snow
      sparkling from facets undisturbed
The earth pristine in winter white
      and no footprints in the snow

Smooth as the glass in a window pane
      no ripple from buried rock or twig
Not etched by traveling bird or beast
      with no footprints in the snow

My heartbeats slow and breath runs out
      my eyes shelter behind their lids
Gone is the cool of leaf and blade bent low
      there are no footprints in the snow

He's left me, the man that brought the warm
      He's left me, the man I loved
Suddenly Death made his claim one morning
      casting no footprints in the snow

He's gone like the flowers, but I'm promised a Spring
      when again we will walk hand in hand
And in the whiteness of the world beyond will we be
      leaving no footprints in the snow?

The mirror
        shows no tint of rose
        no powder will sorrow erase
        here are the windows to a lonely soul
        and the frame of grey about my face

The memory
        of your loving gaze
        when your eyes looked into mine
        they were so tenderly loving me
        I could no dream decline

A soul apart
        you were the spring of endless faith
        you never ceased to offer hope
        my inner me, my grain of self
        was safely folded in your heart's envelope

Gentle one
        I sit here now face to the glass
        behind me the dark empty spaces extend
        the hours crawl until dawn's release
        and to courage and coping I'll pretend

YOUR GRAVE

I went to your grave
    the light of winter sliced bright
And through my tears
    I caressed the cold soil
    seeking you
    marking the spot
    where the marbled stone
        will display
        your years in this world

Pain intensifies
    as I know
    I must wait
    until Eternity
        to see and
        hear you again

Strange in
    losing sight of you
    I sense your love beside me
    and hear you

And the warmth of your memory
    makes it difficult for the cold

73

Albert
>how I love
>>that four-legged
>>>soft-furred
>>>half-blind
>>>animal

Thank you, Harold,
>for your
>>insistence
>>>that he stay
>>>that he be fed
>>>that he be housed

I really did
>not like him then
>>you saw character in those
>>>pointy big ears
>>>clawless paws
>>>hungry cries

Each morning now
>we have our daily chat
>>we comment
>>>to each other
>>>his turn
>>>my turn
>>>we never interrupt
>>>we take our walk
>>>>together
>>>he watches me
>>>>doing my daily tasks

But then
      Emma was here first
                  and lingers on
                  holding what is
                  rightfully hers
                  but an age
                        of twenty years
                        has its effect
                  an acrobat's bones
                        under a tent of fur
                  hunter's teeth
                        lost in the pursuit

I used to worry about her
      until that morning
            she again climbed
                  the huge tree
            and leapt to the peak of
                  the roof

But Albert
      (as always)
      stayed on the ground to
            worry with me

                              p.s. Emma
                                    (as always)
                                    made it back
                                    down

75

WAITING FRIEND

She searched for you
    wherever her blindness
        lead her four feet to
        every corner
        every crevice

    until finally
        she laid down
        to wait
        by the door
        not to miss your entrance

        stubborn
        defensive
        listening

    she could not understand
        her heart broke
        her heart died
        perhaps she thought
            she could find you
            if she just searched elsewhere

    now I wait
        by the door
            stubborn
            defensive
            listening ...

KJO waiting

My heart has ached
    like a rower's arms
    from weariness

My tears
    as tides about grey-black rocks
    have freely flowed

My life
    is submerged in a
    lonely current

Your true love
    was my anchor in life

Your courage
    put Fortune's wind behind me

Your faith
    set buoys into Life's harbor

Your unselfishness
    taught me to share blessings

Through your
    inspired strength and valor

I know that
    in time to come my course

Will follow His plan and
    I will join you again someday

Your grave
    shall
        one of these days
        be more lonely
        than it is today

Your grave so
    tenderly cared for
        began this summer season
          a beard of new grass
          chocolate earth
          daily flowers

But, in time,
    the faithful were
        the yellow plastic
          watering can
            and myself

And the sun finally won
    the green melted into patches
    the sod cracked
    the flowers looked like straw

A record summer of empty hot
    waiting for another prairie winter

Soon you'll be covered
    with the hard wintry ices
        the dry ashen snows

That wooden lair
    and metal nest within
        don't really hold you

I shall carry you
    and your warmth
        within my heart

PRESENT WITH THE PAST

Were my life to float away
        I would not swim after it
For I am unable to call
        you back to me
        the shore is gone

You are beyond my limits
        the hurt will not fade

I touch the hand where your ring remains
        tears gently flow
        like the River of Time passing the place
        where this ring slid on me

STRANDS OF GOLD

You have woven the strands of silver
Now they're memories of polished gold
To weave into your life's tapestry
As the picture begins to unfold

An adventurous voyage of a lifetime's duration
Has been with definite direction
Passing through unavoidable storms
With Faith's and Trust's protection

And now, with Him, you look down the path
To a promise in which all can share
And when you finally reach the Gate
You'll be forgiven for all the error

I SHALL GROW OLD

I plan to live 'til ninety-six
From life, I shall not retire
Should God need my soul
I'll accept, should He desire

My life will be a voyage of faith
Courage and hope strengthened by duty
Completed with love given in knowing
The patience required to cherish beauty

How can I say
    what I mean
    when what I say
        is not what was
        meant to be told?

Am I ridiculous
    am I offensive
    am I then a fool
        or am I growing
        so very old?

LOAN OF TIME

On earth allow me another day
Just a few more hours, Lord, I pray
There's no end to things left undone
Who'll fill these shoes? Can anyone?

There is forgiveness I need to ask
Still left undone is the greater task
Of weaving in a tighter bond
With those of whom I'm ever so fond

Lord, so selfish is my request
Left on earth I shall do my best
Thankful for this time I have now
Then may I enter Heaven somehow

MORE TIME, MORE TIME

My days are so very busy
I have so much to do
That this one lifetime
Simply will not get me through

I need double tomorrows
I need a longer day
For each today becomes a yesterday
The earth revolves and turns away

THERE IS MORE

Old age is an honor
    before death closes all

Though we may
    rise with the dawn
    death may catch
        us unaware

As we place
    our hand in God's
    we tread safely
        into the unknown

    one's earthly life
        lets go
    eternal life
        at last is born

    and there is more
        there is more . . . .

Lord, have you forgotten me?
I have been waiting for Your call
I have lived through this year's seasons
Now again it's turned to Fall

I wish to join those who went before
The ones who meant so much
Lord, I wonder how much longer
Before again I know their touch

My friends I've known for years are grey
The youngsters call me old
My interests fail in what is new
I'm repeating, I am told

I'm certain those who are my family
Are tiring day by day
Of the extra steps they must take
The longer I here stay

I know they love me greatly
They treat me as if I'd break
But, God, I've seen a full, good life
And maybe now my soul You'll take

Nightly between sheet and blanket I lay
I hope, God, to You I'll go
My worldly purpose has been served
Or has it? Only You can know

Life is but a matter of phases
From infancy to golden ages

LET ME DREAM

Let me live the Good Life
I have shared the toil and work
I wish so much to romp and play
Permit me leave and duties shirk

Let me enjoy riches and wealth
I have known well the other side
May my cup now overflow
Silver and gold, power and pride

Let me mingle with the rich
Mine has been the working class
May society heed my status
Record my doings as days pass

Let me become soft from spoils
I have traveled much alone
In comfort I will be kept
May I waste and not atone

Let me ride the waves of ease
Not wanting or in worry
Slowly to glide along the way
Never again called to hurry

Surely these are not my thoughts
The Good Life, so it seems
Happiness surely can never be bought
I have more honest dreams

Hear the words
    as you sing the music

Feel the Spirit
    when you say the prayer

Share the love
    through a confession

Know how to comfort
    when others despair

Behold the beauty
    of Life in a smile

Learn the value
    of a gift of love

Release your compassion
    and forge understanding

For these are God's blessings
    from heaven above

People, brains and computers
      have much under control
However, there are places
      where they'll never play a role

Such as the changing seasons
      the quarters of the year
We must live them as they are
      there's no option here

The months on the calendar
      we could rename
But the monthly realities
      would much stay the same

The wind and the clouds
      convey breeze and storm
The sun's given a task
      that all world be warm

Always will soft leaves be
      the earth's blanket of green
The snow's secret crystals
      two alike have not been seen

The blackness of deep oceans
      the sharp rock of peak's high
Could there be reason
      we would put these awry?

People, brains and computers
      do indeed have vast power
Yet in the time of God's universe
      They are but an hour

Happiness is
the effortless flight of a butterfly
the smile of a daisy in the morning sun
whispered song of love in mid-June
morning mist of an early bright dawn

Happiness dwells in
a father's holding of his child's hand
the dance of starlight on still water
raindrop's splashed gems on a violet petal
treasures in the pockets of a small boy's jeans

Happiness hovers in
the warm air of a bread filled oven
sweet smells of a lavender meadow
scents of a winter's holiday candle
the first bouquet of Spring in a crystal vase

Happiness flourishes among
elders recalling stories of past
the kisses of young lovers parting at the door
lassies in conspiracies of mirth
lads plotting to great and secret ends

Happiness is you and me
Happiness dwells in us
Happiness hovers about us
Happiness flourishes among us
      as we offer
          all this to
              one another

Were I an artist
      this God-given morning

What a colorful scene
      I could put in a frame

With sun, oh so slowly
      arising through tree tops

No two sunrises equal
      They're never the same

Air breathfully clear
      with breezes gently flowing

But eyes need not be open
      nor words to be spoken

To feel God's glory
      swirling about us

Awareness! Life giving!
      and this miracle, a token

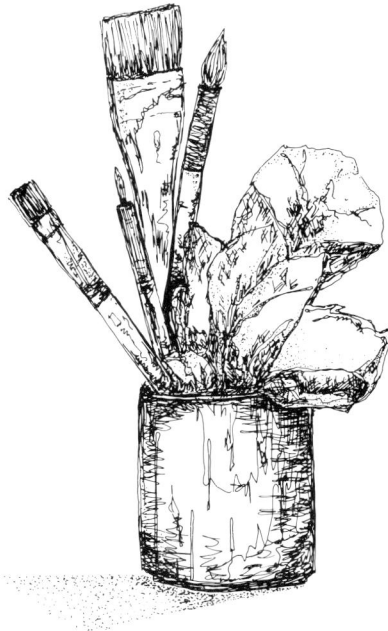

My Lord rains on me care and compassion
Grateful am I to live in this fashion

To wake each morn to daylight bright
To find my path through evening's light

To cherish, to honor and to give
In the way of life I choose to live

To find my quest in love of friends
Flowing in kindness that never ends

These are my whims and wants in prayers
Daily He forgives my constant errors

He is my first and lasting friend
Through Him, life began and shall never end

God has his reason
Our life to season

Beauty to some
Are long, elegant lines
A quiet moment in Nature
Or what the artist refines

Beauty can be learned
In various appreciations
From one's own preference to
The conciousness of nations

Beauty rests in memories
In catacombs of thought
Loved ones now absent
We miss, as we ought

Beauty is living
In hearts and minds unfettered
Thoughtful and tender
With hope of a world bettered

ART OF LISTENING

Listening
    is perfect harmony
        of living
    it intoxicates
        our being
        the more
            we partake

Listening
    hears the songs
        of the birds
    the laugh
        in laughter
    the gentleness
        of love

Listening
    moves the
        cargo of thought
    safe over
        dark waters
            giving and
taking
    a two-way exchange

Listening
    is a valley for
        grief, love and need
    to flow in towards
        our minds
    and flood
        our perception

Our own twitterings
    have lasted a lifetime

Our own thoughts
    have bubbled and soared

We will not
    lose our rightful place
    if we savor
        another's thoughts

We have at last
    heard
        the art of listening

PEACEFUL HAPPINESS

Why am I so happy?
Do I have the right to be?
It seems my world is golden
All this beauty here for me

There is so much for the taking
Nature is a thing all its own
It belongs to us everyone
From lightless depths to cloudy mountain throne

There is pleasure arrayed around us
Family and friends on all sides
The silvered smiles from older faces
The antics on which childhood rides

Elegance resides in the simplest things
Grandeur breaks in dawn's first light
The awareness is a blessing of its own
The joy it brings is a universal right

Each day, when I wake
I thank God I am here
Amidst those I love
Among those I hold dear

All beauty around me
In rapture unfolding
Life is at my fingertips
I reach and I am holding

God has been good
All my family kind
It's their love and needs
Which comfort my mind

The touching and the laughter
Move me to this pray
"Oh, Lord, may I ask for
More time. May I stay?"

Esther and her husband Harold William Asmus

Poems by Esther C. Asmus have appeared in:
Country Messenger
Stillwater Gazette
Our World's Most Beloved Poems
World Poetry Anthology
National Poetry Anthology
Our Western World's Most Beautiful Poems
New American Poetry Anthology

"Esther C. Asmus' book of comfort, advice and challenge has been written from the perspective of personal experience and is infused with wisdom, tact, compassion and profound humanity. Her approach to various topics of life offers a moving and humane understanding, forged by growing experiences. Her writings offer deep insight and invaluable reassurance and uplift."

Pastor Daniel L. Johns
Trinity Lutheran Church
Stillwater, Minnesota